HURRICANES

MICHAEL WOODS AND MARY B. WOODS

LERNER PUBLICATIONS COMPANY
MINNEAPOLIS

To the students, faculty, and staff of the
Benjamin Franklin International School in
Barcelona, Spain

Editor's note: Determining the exact death toll following disasters is often difficult—if not impossible—especially in the case of disasters that took place long ago. The authors and the editors in this series have used their best judgment in determining which figures to include.

Lerner Publications Company
A division of Lerner Publishing Group
241 First Avenue North
Minneapolis, MN 55401 U.S.A.

Website address: www.lernerbooks.com

Library of Congress Cataloging-in-Publication Data

Woods, Michael, 1946–
    Hurricanes / by Michael Woods and Mary B. Woods.
        p.   cm. — (Disasters up close)
    Includes bibliographical references and index.
    ISBN-13: 978–0–8225–4710–5 (lib. bdg. : alk. paper)
    ISBN-10: 0–8225–4710–4 (lib. bdg. : alk. paper)
    1. Hurricanes—Juvenile literature. 2. Storms—Juvenile literature. 3. Disaster victims—Juvenile literature. 4. Disaster relief—Juvenile literature. I. Woods, Mary B. (Mary Boyle), 1946– II. Title. III. Series.
    QC944.2.W66 2007
    363.34'922–dc22   2005032347

Manufactured in the United States of America
1 2 3 4 5 6 – DP – 12 11 10 09 08 07

Contents

Introduction

WHEN HURRICANE KATRINA ROARED THROUGH THE GULF OF MEXICO TOWARD NEW ORLEANS, LOUISIANA, IN 2005, DEBRA ENGLEHART AND HER FAMILY HIT THE ROAD. "WE PACKED A FEW SUITCASES," SAID DEBRA. "WE ONLY EXPECTED TO BE GONE A FEW DAYS. WE NEVER EXPECTED THIS."

This was one of the worst storms in U.S. history. About one million people in Louisiana, Mississippi, and Alabama had to evacuate (leave home for a safer place). Hurricane Katrina did so much damage that hundreds of thousands of people could not go home for months. The hurricane destroyed everything in its path. It wiped out neighborhoods, businesses, schools, and hospitals.

A WALL OF WATER

Katrina hit the Gulf coast with winds of 140 miles (225 kilometers) per hour. The storm ripped apart buildings. It tore down power lines. It snapped trees like matchsticks. Even worse, the winds pushed a giant wall of water onto shore. The wall was more than 25 feet (7 meters) high. It did more damage than the wind or rain.

Everyone feared that Katrina would pass right through New Orleans. Most of its 500,000 residents lived in a bowl-shaped area below sea level. Lake Pontchartrain was on one side. The Mississippi River was on another. To protect the city, levees (high walls) had been built along the river and lake.

When Katrina hit a little to the east, people thought the city had escaped destruction. But they were wrong. Water broke big holes in the levees. Lake Pontchartrain's water poured into the city. At least 80 percent of New Orleans was flooded. The water was 20 feet (6 m) deep in some places.

Hurricane Wilma knocked down power lines in Playa del Carmen, Mexico, in October 2005, two months after Katrina.

4

STRANDED FOR DAYS

Not everyone was able to evacuate before water flowed into New Orleans. Many people had no cars. Others were in hospitals or nursing homes. They had no way of getting out. Still others decided not to evacuate. About forty thousand were stranded for days before help arrived. Helicopters rescued hundreds of people who had to climb on the roofs of their homes to avoid drowning. "I was on the roof for four days," said Adele Bertucci. "I stayed on the roof from early morning, 5:30 or 6, until the roaches and mosquitoes became overbearing."

Katrina killed at least 1,300 people, injured hundreds, and cost about $100 billion in damages. Three weeks later, Hurricane Rita hit the same area with 120-mile-per-hour (193 km/hr) winds and a 15-foot (5 m) wall of water. About 100 people died, hundreds more were injured, and the region suffered at least another $6 billion in damage. Hurricanes Katrina and Rita were large-scale disasters. Disasters are events that cause great destruction.

What Are Hurricanes?

HURRICANES ARE STORMS WITH STRONG, SWIRLING WINDS. THEY CAN BE MORE THAN 300 MILES (483 KM) FROM ONE SIDE TO ANOTHER. THEIR WINDS MAY HOWL AT 200 MILES PER HOUR (322 KM/HR). A HURRICANE MAY LAST FOR WEEKS.

Tornadoes also are storms with swirling winds. Although tornadoes have faster winds, they are smaller than hurricanes and do not last as long. Many are only about 300 yards (274 m) across. They usually last only minutes or a few hours.

Hurricanes also are called tropical cyclones because they form over tropical (warm) ocean waters. A tropical cyclone becomes a hurricane when its wind equals or exceeds 74 miles per hour (119 km/hr).

THE NAME FITS

The word *hurricane* comes from Hurican, a name for the god of evil on some islands in the Caribbean Sea. And like the god, hurricanes can cause a lot of trouble. The worst damage happens when hurricanes move onto the land, in areas where many people live. In 1900 a hurricane in Galveston, Texas, caused the deadliest weather emergency in U.S. history. It killed more than eight thousand people.

A hurricane-damaged ship lies on its side in the Samoan Islands in the late 1800s.

CHOPPY WATERS

Christopher Columbus wrote the first known report of a hurricane. Columbus sailed into the storm in 1495 on one of his voyages to the Americas. It damaged his ships. His crews had to patch together pieces of two ships to sail back home.

"The roof disappeared. The dining room table *flew right out the window.*"

—Robert Moss, remembering the day in 1992 when Hurricane Andrew hit his house in Homestead, Florida

Hurricane Andrew devastated many Florida neighborhoods in 1992.

A hurricane's wind is often destructive. It can blow over trucks and cars. It can tear down electric power lines. It also can damage buildings and roads. Heavy rain adds to the damage. It can cause flooding and mudslides. In a mudslide, soil gets soaked and flows down hills. Helen McCormick will never forget a 1928 hurricane in Florida when she was thirteen years old. "I remember the rain," she said. "I thought it would beat me to death."

STORM SURGE

While wind and rain can be destructive, much of a hurricane's damage comes from storm surge. Storm surge is a huge dome of water that a hurricane sucks up from the ocean. When the hurricane reaches land, the water surges (flows very fast) over everything in its path.

The storm surge in a weak hurricane may pour 3 feet (.9 m) of water over the land. In strong hurricanes, the surge may be more than 25 feet (8 m) high. In 1991 the surge from a storm in Bangladesh killed more than 130,000 people and wrecked millions of homes. Storm surges also can wreck roads, bridges, and farm crops. In 2004 Hurricane Charley's storm surge and flooding damaged about one-third of Florida's orange and grapefruit trees.

ASKING FOR TROUBLE

People do things that can make hurricane disasters worse. In Haiti people use wood for fires to cook their food. They cut trees from hillsides. Tree roots help to hold the soil in place. When Hurricane Jeanne hit Haiti in 2004, its rain turned hillsides into mud. The mud rolled down and buried homes and other buildings (below).

In Florida and other coastal states, people build expensive homes and hotels near the shore. The buildings are directly in the path of hurricanes. These risky building practices increase the likelihood of hurricane damage.

In October 2005, massive waves from Hurricane Wilma crashed over a sea wall in Havana, Cuba. The storm surge flooded neighborhoods near the shore and caused millions of dollars in damage.

MORE 'CANES?

The number of hurricanes that form each year depends on conditions in the oceans. These conditions include water temperatures and currents (areas of water that flow like great rivers). In an average year, about six Atlantic Ocean hurricanes occur. Only one or two hit land on the U.S.

Part of this Florida mobile home was lodged in a tree after Hurricane Jeanne pounded the East Coast in late 2004.

Atlantic coast or Gulf of Mexico. But the number of Atlantic hurricanes began to rise in 1995. The 2005 Atlantic hurricane season was the worst ever. The Atlantic coast region saw fifteen hurricanes in the 2005 season—more than in any season since record keeping began. In addition, the season produced Hurricane Katrina. Katrina caused more damage than any other hurricane in history.

Some scientists think the rise in hurricanes is due to a natural cycle (pattern). Hurricanes are rare for the first thirty to sixty years of the cycle. Then they become more common for the next thirty to sixty years. Other scientists blame global warming. Global warming is an increase in Earth's temperature due to air pollution. When Earth's temperature rises, so do temperatures in the oceans. Warm ocean temperatures give hurricanes energy.

If scientists are right about global warming, the world could continue to see more hurricanes than it has in the past. Scientists do not know whether more hurricanes will also hit land. If that happens, hurricane disasters also could become more common.

ARE YOU A HURRICANE?

Check for your name on the latest list of hurricane names at http://www.nhc.noaa .gov/aboutnames.shtml

Hurricane Ivan ripped the front wall off this clothing store in Pensacola, Florida, in 2004.

1780
HURRICANE IN THE CARIBBEAN

A gentle day on the island of Barbados. Barbados has not experienced major hurricane damage since 1955.

When stormy weather arrived on October 10, 1780, many people on the island of Barbados in the Caribbean Sea probably didn't worry about a disaster. *"There had been nothing that could be called a hurricane felt at Barbados for more than a century before 1780,"* Dr. Gilbert Blane later wrote. This storm made up for it—and much more.

The deadliest Atlantic hurricane ever recorded hit Barbados. Then it ripped through other islands in the Caribbean Sea with terrible strength. The storm's winds may have been greater than 200 miles per hour (323 km/hr). The winds inside the hurricane were fast. But the storm itself moved slowly. Wind and rain pounded the area for days.

Sir George Rodney described the damage on Barbados in a letter. *"The strongest buildings and the whole of the houses, most of which were stone, and remarkable for their solidity, gave*

12

way to the fury of the wind, and were torn up. . . . Had I not been an eyewitness, nothing could have induced me to have believed it," he wrote. The wind and water acted like a lawn mower. They cut down trees and stripped plants from the ground. Where there once was vegetation, only bare land remained.

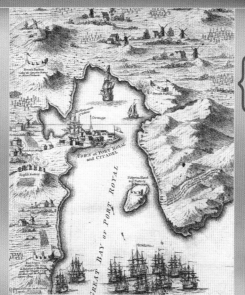

This 1825 map shows Port Royal, Martinique, another Caribbean island damaged by the 1780 hurricane.

The hurricane happened during the American Revolutionary War (1775–1783). British and French warships were in the Caribbean. The storm hit them hard. It destroyed eight British warships. More than forty French ships carrying four thousand soldiers sank. Many fishing boats also sank, and their crews drowned.

Some of the islands had forts built by the British and French. A British soldier went to Barbados to check on the damage. He reported that an earthquake had happened along with the hurricane. He could not believe that wind and water alone had caused such damage on the island.

About twenty-two thousand people died in the storm. More suffering and death happened in the days following the hurricane. The wind and water destroyed food crops and farm animals, so many people had nothing to eat. A large number of those who starved to death were slaves—people who performed hard labor on the islands. These people had no power or money. They had no way of getting food or water after the hurricane hit.

In addition to hitting Barbados, the storm caused extreme damage on the islands of Saint Lucia, Martinique, Dominica, Saint Eustatius, and Puerto Rico. The Western Hemisphere would not experience a storm of similar strength until 1900, when a hurricane slammed into Galveston Island in Texas.

"[The trees] were stripped of their bark."

—Dr. Gilbert Blane, describing the island of Barbados after a 1780 hurricane

What Causes Hurricanes?

HURRICANES NEED HEAT AND MOISTURE TO FORM. THEY USUALLY ARE BORN OVER WARM, TROPICAL OCEANS, WHERE THOSE CONDITIONS EXIST. MOST ATLANTIC OCEAN HURRICANES START ON THE WEST COAST OF AFRICA. THEN THEY MOVE WEST TOWARD THE UNITED STATES.

Warm ocean water supplies the energy for a hurricane's wind. Warm, moist air above the water rises upward from the ocean surface. An area of low pressure (rising air) forms underneath. Nearby air rushes into the low-pressure area and produces winds. The ocean also provides moisture for a hurricane's rain. Ocean water evaporates, changing into a gas called water vapor. The air absorbs that moisture, which later will fall as rain.

Hurricanes form over tropical oceans such as the Pacific above.

GIVE IT A TWIST!

Earth's rotation gives the winds a twist. In the Northern Hemisphere, it makes wind swirl in a counterclockwise direction. In the Southern Hemisphere, these winds rotate clockwise.

As the air rises, it cools. Cooling water vapor turns back into drops of liquid. The drops form clouds and release heat energy that keeps air rising and winds swirling. As long as a hurricane stays near warm water, plenty of energy exists to keep it strong.

Hurricanes usually weaken when they reach land. Their energy supply is cut off. There is no warm water over the land. Strong winds higher in the atmosphere also can weaken a hurricane or blow it apart.

A man is caught off guard as a massive storm surge crashes onto a Florida beach during a hurricane in 1947.

GOING THROUGH A STAGE

Hurricanes go through four stages. They begin as tropical disturbances. Then they strengthen into tropical depressions. When the wind in a tropical depression moves faster than 38 miles per hour (61 km/hr), the depression becomes a tropical storm.

Meteorologists (scientists who study the weather) give each tropical storm a name. The name sticks with the storm if it strengthens into a hurricane. Hurricane Charley in 2004, for instance, began as Tropical Storm Charley.

A storm becomes a hurricane when its winds equal or exceed 74 miles per hour (119 km/hr). When hurricanes weaken after reaching land, they become tropical storms and tropical depressions once again.

Damaged boats piled onshore after Hurricane Hugo tore through South Carolina in 1989.

HIS-A-CANES

Until the 1950s, hurricanes had no official names. That caused confusion. If several hurricanes hit the same area, people couldn't tell one from another. At first, hurricanes got only women's names. The World Meteorological Organization (WMO), part of the United Nations, added men's names in 1979.

WMO makes up six lists of hurricane and tropical storm names. They include names popular in each part of the world where hurricanes occur. The names are in alphabetical order. Each year WMO uses one of the six lists. In the sixth year, the lists began repeating. The 2007 list will be reused in 2013.

In 2005 so many storms occurred that forecasters used all twenty-one names. When that happens, they use letters of the Greek alphabet. This alphabet starts with letters called alpha, beta, and gamma.

STORM WITH AN EYE

Weather forecasters take pictures of hurricanes from satellites. Satellites are small, unmanned spacecraft. They circle high above Earth's surface. Satellite pictures show a hurricane's core, or eye. The eye is a big swirl of clouds with a hole in the center. It is very calm in the middle of the eye. Little wind or rain is there.

A hurricane's strongest winds occur in the eyewall. The eyewall is a bank of swirling clouds that surrounds the eye. The eyewall sucks up ocean water for the storm surge, like a drinking straw. Great disasters can occur when the eyewall passes directly through a city. Winds in the eyewall increase as the eye gets smaller and decrease when the eye gets wider.

Bands of clouds swirl out from the eyewall. These clouds are called rainbands. Rain gets very heavy when a rainband is overhead. Rain gets lighter in between rainbands.

Weather satellites give scientists clear views of hurricanes. The image above shows Hurricane Linda approaching California in 1997, while the image at right charts Hurricane Fran's path toward North Carolina in 1996.

INSIDE A HURRICANE

storm clouds

eyewall

eye

spiraling winds

MONSTER STORMS

Hurricanes move slowly from one place to another. They may travel only 10 or 20 miles per hour (16 or 32 km/hr). A hurricane can last for only a few days or for several weeks. Hurricanes that last a long time can travel far. Hurricane Faith lasted for fifteen days in 1966 and traveled 7,500 miles (12,070 km).

Hurricanes vary in size. Many are about 300 miles (483 km) from one side to another. Smaller storms, however, can be just as dangerous. Hurricane Andrew in 1992 was only about 40 miles (64 km) across. But it caused $25 billion in damage.

A hurricane may get stronger when moving through warm water and weaken over colder water. Hurricanes also may weaken if they encounter strong winds blowing high in the atmosphere. The winds can blow a hurricane apart.

Hurricane Andrew caused extensive damage throughout Florida in 1992.

BYE-BYE NAMES

When a hurricane causes a great disaster, its name is retired. The name is not used again for ten years. The first three male names ever used for hurricanes—Bob, David, and Frederick—all were retired.

> "The house just **filled up with water.**
> It **forced me into the attic**
> and then I ended up kicking out the wall
> and climbing out to a tree."

—Mike Spencer, recalling his attempts to escape the rising water in Gulfport, Mississippi, after Hurricane Katrina in 2005

An aerial view of the flooding in New Orleans, Louisiana, after Hurricane Katrina caused Lake Pontchartrain and the Mississippi River to breach (overflow) their levees.

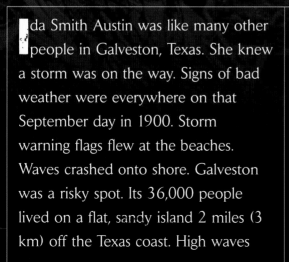

1900
THE HURRICANE
THAT
ATE GALVESTON

A woman walks along a path cleared of hurricane debris.

Ida Smith Austin was like many other people in Galveston, Texas. She knew a storm was on the way. Signs of bad weather were everywhere on that September day in 1900. Storm warning flags flew at the beaches. Waves crashed onto shore. Galveston was a risky spot. Its 36,000 people lived on a flat, sandy island 2 miles (3 km) off the Texas coast. High waves could wash right over the city.

On September 8, Austin was working around her house. Galveston often had storms. She wasn't even thinking about this one. Suddenly, she heard a man yelling as he ran past her house. Puzzled, Austin went out to her porch. Water was pouring down the street. Soon it flooded her front yard and kept

A house lay on its side after floodwaters from the Galveston hurricane swept through.

coming. A great hurricane had arrived. It began to eat Galveston.

"In an incredibly short time the water surged [o]ver the [porch] driven by a furiously blowing wind," Austin recalled. *"Trees began to fall, slate shingles, planks and debris of every imaginable kind were being hurled through the air. . . . Ten very large trees were soon uprooted and fell crashing, banging, and scraping against our house. We opened all downstairs [doors] and let the water flow through. Soon it stood 3 feet [.9 m] in all the rooms."*

Austin's house was damaged, but she survived. Many other people were not so lucky. The 1900 hurricane caused the worst weather disaster in U.S. history. It brought 150-mile-per-hour (241 km/hr) winds and a storm surge about 20 feet (6 m) high. The whole island flooded. Waves crashed into buildings and tore them apart. One was an orphanage where ninety children and all the teachers died.

"The roofs of houses and timbers were flying through the streets as though they were paper," Isaac M.

"Everything was swept away and nearly all drowned."

—John D. Blagden, describing the 1900 Galveston hurricane

Cline wrote in a report. He worked in Galveston's U.S. Weather Bureau office. Cline's own wife died when their house collapsed in the storm.

John D. Blagden stayed at work in the weather bureau office during the hurricane. The next day, he left his workplace. Blagden walked through block after block of smashed houses. Dead bodies were all around. *"I could not even find the place where I had been staying,"* he said.

The 1900 hurricane killed more than eight thousand people and wrecked half the homes in Galveston. In one area where twenty thousand people lived, every house was destroyed.

23

Hurricane Country

A Florida house was buried in sand from Hurricane Ivan's storm surge in 2004.

HURRICANES OCCUR IN MANY PARTS OF THE WORLD. MOST FORM IN THE ATLANTIC OCEAN, PACIFIC OCEAN, AND INDIAN OCEAN. HURRICANES CAUSE THE WORST TROUBLE FOR PEOPLE WHO LIVE ALONG COASTS.

However, hurricanes also can cause disasters farther inland. When a hurricane passes over land, its winds get weaker. But the storm still can drop large amounts of rain. In 2004 Ivan dumped almost 6 inches (16 centimeters) of rain on Pittsburgh, Pennsylvania, in twenty-four hours. "The whole town's wrecked," said Bill Wotkutch, who helped his parents clean up their home in the nearby town of Millvale. Ivan flooded the house and destroyed neighboring buildings.

TIRELESS STORM

Hurricane/Typhoon John lasted longer than any other hurricane in history. It huffed and puffed for thirty-one days in August and September of 1994. John was both a hurricane and a typhoon because it moved through both eastern and western parts of the Pacific Ocean.

DIFFERENT NAMES, SAME STORMS

Hurricanes have different names in different areas. Only storms that form in the North Atlantic Ocean, Caribbean Sea, the Gulf of Mexico, and the northeastern Pacific Ocean are called hurricanes. The same storms are called typhoons when they form near the Philippines or in the China Sea. Near Australia and in the Indian Ocean, these storms are called cyclones.

24

Hurricanes move after they form. They usually travel slowly. In the Northern Hemisphere, Earth's rotation makes hurricanes drift toward the North Pole. In the Southern Hemisphere, they drift toward the South Pole.

HURRICANE SEASON

Most hurricanes occur in the summer and fall, when the ocean water is warm. In the Atlantic Ocean, Caribbean Sea, and Gulf of Mexico, hurricanes usually happen between June 1 and November 30. This period is called hurricane season. August and September are the peak of hurricane season.

In Australia and the Indian Ocean, cyclone season runs from December to March. The seasons are reversed in the Southern Hemisphere, so summer begins in December. In the northwest Pacific Ocean, most typhoons occur in the summer.

HURRICANE ALLEY

Unlike tornadoes and other severe storms, hurricanes seldom cause great disasters right where they form. Trouble occurs when hurricanes approach the land. Some areas of the United States are directly in the path that Atlantic hurricanes usually follow. The states most often hit by hurricanes are on the East Coast. They run all the way from Texas to Maine.

Hurricanes often make landfall (come onto the shore) along the southeastern coast of the United States or the Gulf of Mexico. However, they can make landfall much farther north. One of the worst natural disasters in U.S. history happened in 1938 when a hurricane came ashore in the New England states.

THE PERFECT STORM

At the end of October in 1991, a terrible storm hit the eastern United States. Some people called it the Halloween Storm—and it *was* spooky. Three storms, including Hurricane Grace, appeared just at the right time. They joined together to make a monster. Waves 100 feet (30 m) high and winds of 120 miles per hour (193 km/hr) sank ships and battered the shore from North Carolina and South Carolina to Nova Scotia in Canada. A man named Sebastian Junger helped make this storm famous. He described it in a book called *The Perfect Storm*.

DISASTER ZONES

Hurricanes occur on coasts around the world. This map shows just a few of Earth's most severe hurricanes. Many storms featured on the map do not have names. That is because different regions of the world have different systems for naming storms—and some regions did not start naming storms until recently. The U.S. National Weather Service began assigning women's names to Atlantic storms in 1953. Storms that form in the Bay of Bengal, near India, did not receive names until 2004.

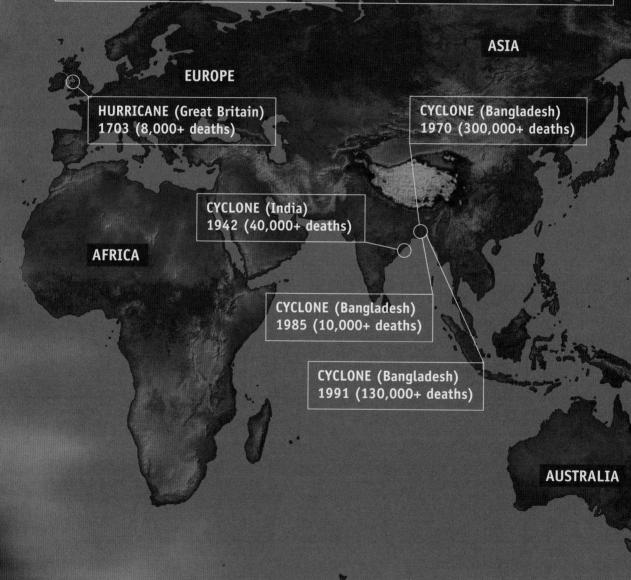

ASIA

EUROPE

HURRICANE (Great Britain)
1703 (8,000+ deaths)

CYCLONE (Bangladesh)
1970 (300,000+ deaths)

CYCLONE (India)
1942 (40,000+ deaths)

AFRICA

CYCLONE (Bangladesh)
1985 (10,000+ deaths)

CYCLONE (Bangladesh)
1991 (130,000+ deaths)

AUSTRALIA

HURRICANE (East Coast)
1938 (500+ deaths)

NORTH AMERICA

HURRICANE CAMILLE (Mississippi,
Lousiana, West Virgina, Virgina)
1969 (200+ deaths)

HURRICANE (Caribbean)
1780 (22,000+ deaths)

HURRICANE KATRINA (Gulf coast)
2005 (1,300+ deaths)

HURRICANE (Galveston, Texas)
1900 (8,000+ deaths)

HURRICANE (Florida)
1928 (2,000+ deaths)

HURRICANE STAN
(Mexico and Central America)
2005 (1,200+ deaths)

SOUTH AMERICA

Waves crash onto shore in Woods Hole, Massachusetts, during a 1938 hurricane.

1938
THE GREAT NEW ENGLAND HURRICANE

Arthur Raynor was worried about the weather on September 21, 1938. He noticed that the birds in his grandmother's yard on Long Island, New York, were acting strangely. Could their behavior mean a storm was on its way?

Raynor asked his grandmother and her mother, who was at the house for a visit. But they answered with their usual reply, he recalled: *"One thing you never have to worry about on Long Island is floods, hurricanes, earthquakes and all those other things everybody not smart enough to live here worry about."*

But sometimes adults can be wrong. For a great storm was about to hit. It was one of the area's worst hurricanes in the twentieth century. After a twelve-day journey across the Atlantic Ocean, the no-name storm came onshore near Raynor's hometown. Then it headed north into the New England states.

The storm surge was more than 20 feet (6 m) high in some areas. **"As we [drove] down the hill at Oneck Lane, about 3 feet [.9 m] of water shot across the road in front of us,"** Raynor remembered. In cities from New York to Maine, floods washed away buildings, docks, roads, and railroad tracks. Providence, Rhode Island, almost disappeared under 20 feet (6 m) of water. Water 8 feet (2 m) deep rushed through Falmouth and New Bedford, Massachusetts.

It swept Betty Mills, twelve, right out of her house. Mills saved herself by hanging onto wreckage floating in the water. Then she swam to dry land. Floods, waves, and winds that reached 125 miles per hour (201 km/hr) tore buildings apart and knocked down power lines. The storm knocked down about two *billion* trees in New England.

In Connecticut fallen power lines sparked and set off huge fires. Throughout the disaster area, about 20,000 miles (32,187 km) of power lines and telephone wires were knocked down. The hurricane wrecked about twenty-six thousand cars. About nine thousand homes and other buildings were destroyed and fifteen thousand damaged in the storm.

Richard K. Hawes watched as wind and water hit the homes of families he knew in Westport, Massachusetts. **"The Welsh house seemed to rise bodily in the air and turn completely over,"** he reported.

The waves that struck the seawall during the New England hurricane looked like erupting geysers.

" *The Thatcher house seemed to burst apart.* "
—*Richard K. Hawes, a witness to the 1938 New England hurricane*

Farmers lost 750,000 chickens, almost two thousand cows, and half of New England's famous crop of apples. Almost six thousand fishing boats were sunk or carried inland and smashed against the ground. The hurricane killed 564 people. At least 1,700 people were seriously injured.

Measuring Hurricanes

WHEN PEOPLE HEAR THAT A HURRICANE IS COMING, THEY ASK, "HOW DANGEROUS IS IT?" FORTUNATELY, METEOROLOGISTS OFTEN CAN ANSWER THAT QUESTION BEFORE A HURRICANE ARRIVES. THEY FIND THE ANSWER WITH THE SAFFIR-SIMPSON HURRICANE SCALE. THIS SCALE DOES NOT WEIGH A HURRICANE. RATHER, IT SHOWS THE AMOUNT OF DAMAGE A HURRICANE COULD CAUSE.

Meteorologists can make predictions about the strength of hurricanes because the storms last long enough to take measurements. A hurricane may swirl over ocean waters for days before making landfall. As a result, meteorologists can determine how strong a hurricane is before the storm affects many people's lives.

SAFFIR-SIMPSON SCALE

Herbert Saffir and Robert Simpson invented the hurricane scale in 1969. Saffir was an engineer. He studied wind damage from hurricanes. Simpson was the director of the National Hurricane Center, which predicts hurricanes.

The Saffir-Simpson Hurricane Scale assigns categories, or numbers, to each hurricane. The categories let people know how strong upcoming storms might be.

A Florida bridge is filled with bumper-to-bumper traffic as people evacuate in anticipation of Hurricane Charley in 2004.

Hurricane Mitch caused extensive flood damage in Honduras *(above)* and other Central American countries.

"The road through our village **had turned into an enormous river.**

Clothes, furniture, food, and belongings were **all being taken away.**"

—Marian Acuna Cruz, describing the effects of Hurricane Mitch in 1998 near her home in the Central American country of Nicaragua

When people know that an upcoming hurricane will be weak, they may decide to stay home. When warnings call for a strong hurricane, people may choose to head out. Schools and businesses may close as well. The ability to predict a hurricane's strength saves lives. It also saves people from evacuating needlessly.

PICK A NUMBER

Category 1 hurricanes are the weakest. They have winds of 74 to 95 miles per hour (119 to 153 km/hr). They have storm surges of 4 to 5 feet (1.2–1.5 m). They can cause some flooding. But they cause little or no damage to buildings. Hurricane Otis in 2005 was a Category 1 storm when it struck Mexico.

Category 5 hurricanes are the strongest storms. Winds howl at more than 155 miles per hour (249 km/hr). The storm surge can be at least 18 feet (5.4 m). Bad flooding inland and serious damage to wooden buildings would occur. Hurricane Mitch in 1998 was a Category 5 storm.

Category 3, 4, and 5 hurricanes are major storms. Fortunately, they are rare. In an average hurricane season, two to four major hurricanes occur. Not all reach the land.

Hurricane Katrina was still a Category 1 hurricane when it hit Florida's coast in 2005. Therefore, many people did not evacuate and had to battle high winds, driving rain, and flying debris.

KNOWING ABOUT NOAA

The National Oceanic and Atmospheric Administration (NOAA) is an agency of the U.S. government. NOAA's National Hurricane Center in Miami, Florida, predicts hurricanes. NOAA also picks the Saffir-Simpson category for each hurricane. The National Weather Service is part of NOAA. It forecasts other weather conditions.

THE SAFFIR-SIMPSON HURRICANE SCALE

CATEGORY	WINDS	STORM SURGE
1	74-95 MILES PER HOUR (119-153 KM/HR)	GENERALLY 4-5 FEET (1.2-1.5 M) ABOVE NORMAL
2	96-110 MILES PER HOUR (154-177 KM/HR)	GENERALLY 6-8 FEET (1.8-2.4 M) ABOVE NORMAL
3	111-130 MILES PER HOUR (178-209 KM/HR)	GENERALLY 9-12 FEET (2.7-3.6 M) ABOVE NORMAL
4	131-155 MILES PER HOUR (210-249 KM/HR)	GENERALLY 13-18 FEET (3.9-5.4 M) ABOVE NORMAL
5	GREATER THAN 155 MILES PER HOUR (249 KM/RH)	GENERALLY GREATER THAN 18 FEET (5.4 M) ABOVE NORMAL

In 1954 Hurricane Carol destroyed hundreds of summer cottages on the Connecticut coast.

HURRICANE HUNTERS

Meteorologists use several kinds of technology to measure a hurricane's strength. U.S. Air Force planes called Hurricane Hunters take some of the most accurate storm measurements. These planes are very strong. They can fly right into hurricanes. Flying into a hurricane is bumpy. But the flights are quite safe.

Hurricane Hunters drop packages of instruments that record data about a hurricane. The packages sink down through the storm. Called dropwindsondes, the instruments tell meteorologists about the wind speed, temperature, and atmospheric pressure inside a hurricane. Low-pressure measurements are especially important. They mean that the storm has strong winds. Hurricane Wilma in 2005 had the lowest pressure ever measured for a hurricane in the Atlantic Ocean.

Dropwindsondes measure storms for only a split second as they fall through the air. A newer instrument—called the Stepped Frequency Microwave Radiometer—gives continuous readings. This sensor measures electronic signals given off by a storm. It then uses them to show wind speeds.

NOAA's P-3 aircraft flies above the eye of Hurricane Caroline in 1975.

A researcher sits at his workstation aboard the NOAA WP-3D Orion aircraft. He was studying Hurricane Ophelia in September 2005.

A boy stands among the ruins of his village in Bangladesh.

1991
SUPER CYCLONE
IN BANGLADESH

Bangladesh is a flat country near India. Located on the Bay of Bengal, its land is only a little higher than water in the bay. About 140 million people live close together on a small amount of land. Most live in huts made from dried mud and straw that can fall apart when soaked by rain.

No wonder cyclones often cause great disasters there. One struck on April 29, 1991. With wind roaring at 145 miles per hour (233 km/hr), it pushed a wall of water over Bangladesh. People knew that a storm was coming. The weather had been wet and windy for days. But they got only a few hours of advance warning that the storm was a terrible cyclone.

Some people found shelter in sturdy buildings. As the water rose, others had to stand on the roofs of their houses. People climbed trees and sat in them for days while the water swirled below. Those swept away grabbed for tree branches, cows, and other floating objects to keep their heads above the muddy water.

Eight-year-old Asel Haider was at home when the cyclone hit. **"My father went outside and the wind tore the hair from his head,"** Haider remembered. His family went to bed around midnight. **"An hour later, the water poured in. . . ."** Haider said. **"I didn't know if I was in my house or at sea."**

The water swept Haider into a coconut tree. When morning came, he looked around. **"Everyone was naked,"** Haider said. **"Our clothes had been torn off by the wind. My mother was crying because my baby brother had been pulled from her lap by the water and she didn't know where he was."**

The cyclone killed more than 130,000 people. It destroyed the homes where 10 million people once lived. Many people in this poor country raised cows for milk and meat. The cyclone killed 500,000 of these

Floodwaters from the Bangladesh cyclone cover fields in Chittagong.

precious animals. Crops died as 6 feet (2 m) of water covered farmers' fields. The cyclone left people in Bangladesh homeless and hungry.

Jotish Chandra Koibarta survived the 1991 disaster. But he remembered an even worse cyclone that hit Bangladesh in 1970. When the storm began, his family had huddled on high ground and hoped the water wouldn't reach them. But the waves had risen higher and higher. His wife and 4 children had drowned. The 1970 cyclone killed about 300,000 people in Bangladesh. It was the most destructive storm ever to strike the country.

" *I saw my family being* **washed away** *before my eyes.* "

—Jotish Chandra Koibarta, describing his experience in a cyclone

People Helping People

IN MOST DISASTERS, RELIEF AND RECOVERY WORK STARTS WHEN THE DAMAGE IS DONE. RELIEF MEANS REDUCING THE AMOUNT OF SUFFERING AMONG PEOPLE INVOLVED IN A DISASTER. RECOVERY MEANS HELPING PEOPLE GET THEIR LIVES BACK TO NORMAL. RELIEF WORK FOR HURRICANES OFTEN STARTS BEFORE THE STORM CAUSES ANY DAMAGE.

When a hurricane is on its way, many people must evacuate. These people need places to stay, food, water, medical help, and bathrooms. Disaster relief organizations such as the American Red Cross provide these things.

City, state, and national governments also help. They set up shelters during hurricane evacuations. Shelters often are in schools. Families can sleep on cots lined up in the gym. They can eat hot meals from the cafeteria.

Residents in Florida board up an office building in preparation for Hurricane Wilma in 2005.

BEFORE AND AFTER WORK

People also help themselves and their neighbors before a hurricane hits. In the days before they evacuate, people often try to reduce the amount of damage to their homes and businesses. They place sheets of wood over windows to keep the glass from breaking. They put bags of sand around doorways to keep floodwaters from getting inside. They remove porch chairs from their yards so the wind won't blow them around.

People also prepare for life after returning home. For the first few days, there may be no electricity or water. Everyone buys food and flashlights. They pick up extra batteries and bottled water. They fill their bathtubs too.

That way they'll have water to use for cleaning. Gas stations are busy before a hurricane. Pumps at filling stations will not work when the power is out.

DISASTER ZONE!

When people return home, they may get a nice surprise. The storm may have been weaker than expected, or maybe it took a different path. Their homes are still standing. Life can get back to normal.

But people also may return to a disaster zone. And if they do, they need help to recover. "The worst part of the hurricane was when we came out of the closet we were in and saw there was nothing left," said Michael Benitez. He was a young boy when Hurricane Andrew hit in 1992. "The house had only three walls and a roof." "We survived the storm and now we are struggling to survive the aftermath," said Marilyn Wallace, who was in Hurricane Katrina.

Beds, couches, and carpets may be wet and dirty. Many people need help cleaning their homes or removing ruined possessions. "After the water leaves, you've got black mud about four to five inches high—stinking black mud that you've got to get out of your house," said Marie Peralta. Hurricane Camille wrecked her house in 1969. With the electricity off, milk and other food in the fridge might be rotten. People need cool drinks to prevent dehydration. They also may want to seek shelter in a place with running water and air conditioning. In warm climates, people can suffer heat strokes when the power goes out after a

THE STRONGEST STORM

Hurricane Camille *(below)* in 1969 was the strongest hurricane to hit the United States. When the eye came ashore over Mississippi, winds reached 200 miles per hour (322 km/hr), and the storm surge was 25 feet (7 m) high. Camille caused about 200 deaths.

A family in the Caribbean island nation of the Dominican Republic eats a meal in their flooded, roofless home after Hurricane David passed in 1980.

MONEY TO REBUILD

Hurricane victims need money to fix their homes or find new places to live. In the United States, many people get money from insurance companies. Homeowners who live in hurricane zones pay money each month to insurance companies. If their homes are damaged, these companies give the people money to fix them.

The U.S. government also provides hurricane victims with money to help repair damage and rebuild. Many relief organizations, including the Red Cross, also may help. The Red Cross uses money donated by people outside the disaster zone.

Donations of time and money are helpful to people who survive a disaster. After four strong hurricanes struck Florida in 2004, many people were able to get their lives back just months after the storms. Their homes were repaired or were being rebuilt. People donated supplies and took part in cleanup efforts.

People around the world pitched in again when Hurricane Katrina struck in 2005. But then, the damage was so bad that many could not return for months. Families around the country opened their homes to the disaster victims. Relief agencies helped them find new homes, schools, and jobs. Some never returned to New Orleans. Instead, they began new lives in other parts of the country. Others are still searching for new homes.

FAMOUS RELIEF WORKER

Clara Barton *(right)*, who started the American Red Cross, personally led the team of relief workers for the great 1900 hurricane in Galveston, Texas. News traveled slowly in those days. It took almost two days for the Red Cross to learn about the disaster.

Barton was seventy-eight years old. Nevertheless, she worked with a Red Cross relief team for three months. The team nursed people who were hurt and sick and gave food to thousands of Galveston people.

Thousands of Hurricane Katrina
victims found temporary shelter at
the Houston, Texas, Astrodome.

TENT CITIES

Recovery from a hurricane can take even longer in poor cities and countries. Planes and trucks loaded with food, water, and medicine started arriving in Haiti after Hurricane Jeanne in 2004. The supplies came from the U.S. government, the Red Cross, CARE International, and other organizations that help in disasters. Relief organizations stepped in again in 2005 when Hurricane Katrina hit New Orleans.

"The good news is that we've reached more than 22,000 people," Abby Maxman, of CARE, said about relief work in Haiti in 2004. "But there are at the very least 100,000 more in need." It can take longer to recover in developing countries because people often have no money to rebuild their homes and lives. The governments also are poor and cannot afford to offer much help.

Disaster victims often must live in tents. After Hurricane Jeanne, relief workers started building a tent city for the 300,000 people who lost their homes. Tents may be the only home people have after big hurricanes in poor countries.

EAT YOUR MREs, CHILDREN

A Meal, Ready-To-Eat (MRE) is a full meal in a sealed plastic bag *(below)*. The U.S. government invented MREs for soldiers. But relief workers may pass them out to disaster victims.

The twenty-four different MRE menus include some for vegetarians (people who don't eat meat). The main course may be beef stew or a veggie burger with all the trimmings. Dessert may be a fudge brownie or cake.

You can eat your MRE cold or pop the sealed bag into boiling water. The package also contains a little flameless heater to warm the food.

MEAL, READY-TO-EAT, INDIVIDUAL
DO NOT ROUGH HANDLE WHEN FROZEN
(0 degrees Fahrenheit or below)

A couple sits with what few possession they
have left amid the ruins of their home after
Hurricane Jeanne swept through Haiti in 2004.

The Pantaleon River washes over a road linking two cities in Guatemala after Hurricane Stan.

2005
HURRICANE STAN

Stan was not a strong storm. It was only a Category 1 hurricane, the weakest kind, when it reached the coast of Mexico and Central America in October 2005. Stan got even weaker when it passed over land. As the winds dropped to about 50 miles per hour (65 km/hr), Stan became just a tropical storm.

Thousands of people had fled their homes as Stan approached. They remembered Hurricane Katrina and Hurricane Rita. Just a few weeks earlier, those hurricanes caused a disaster for their neighbors living across the Gulf of Mexico in the United States. Stan's wind, they thought, wasn't going to flatten their houses. So some of them felt a little silly for leaving.

But it wasn't the wind that turned southern Mexico, Nicaragua, Honduras, Guatemala, and El Salvador into a disaster zone. It was the rain. And the mud.

Stan dumped 20 inches (50 cm) of rain on some of those areas. Rain soaked into the soil on the many hillsides. Soon the soil could not soak up any more water. The rain turned whole hills into mud.

As more rain poured down, massive landslides and mudslides occurred. Huge sheets of mud started sliding down the hills. Imagine rivers of mud as wide as football fields! They poured right into the many villages built at the bottom of the hills.

Many people who did not evacuate were buried under the mud. Mud also knocked down bridges and blocked roads. About 300,000 people who lived in villages in Mexico's countryside were cut off from the rest of the world. They could not get out. And rescue and relief workers could not get in to help.

Stan's clouds and heavy rain made it impossible for helicopters and airplanes to fly in water, food, and medicine. The stranded people waited for days for help to arrive. **"The situation is more than critical,"** remarked Raul Murillo, an emergency official in El Salvador.

Rain was the big problem in other areas. In Guatemala, for instance, floods

"It rained entire rivers."

—Beatriz Aguilar, who was in El Salvador when Hurricane Stan hit in 2005

more than 6 feet (2 m) deep destroyed hundreds of homes, stores, schools, and other buildings. More than twenty-four thousand people from 270 villages had to leave home and stay in shelters.

"In some cases, entire communities have been destroyed, leaving families buried," said Carlos Rosales, a relief worker in Guatemala.

Stan caused at least 1,200 deaths— almost as many as Hurricane Katrina. Hundreds of people were injured. Many thousands lost their homes.

The relentless rain that followed Hurricane Stan flooded rivers, causing mudslides and washing out homes (left). Rescue workers retrieved many dead bodies from the wreckage (above).

The Future

IN 1997 A CYCLONE HIT BANGLADESH. IT WAS JUST AS STRONG AS EARLIER STORMS, INCLUDING A 1985 CYCLONE THAT KILLED ABOUT 10,000 BANGLADESHIS. "[O]NLY 127 PEOPLE DIED," SAID MONOWAR HOSSAIN AKHAND, A GOVERNMENT WORKER IN BANGLADESH.

What happened to save so many lives? Monowar said that fewer people died in the storm because the government took extra safety measures. For a long time, everyone knew that Bangladesh needed cyclone shelters where people would be safe from the storms.

Most people in Bangladesh are poor. They live in houses made from mud blocks. The houses fall apart easily during heavy rain. Cyclone shelters are strong buildings. They sit on columns 12 feet (4 m) high. When a cyclone strikes, people can go to the shelter. They will be safe from its storm surge and wind.

In 1991 the shelters had room for only 350,000 people. More than 3 million people needed a safe place. Bangladesh built new shelters throughout the 1990s. The new shelters have room for thousands more people. And when the weather is good, people can use the shelters for meetings and classes.

EARLY WARNING SYSTEMS

Officials also set up an early warning system. It broadcasts alerts on radio and television so people know when to seek shelter. Thousands of volunteers warn people who do not have radio or television so they can go to shelters too.

Most of this village was destroyed in the 1991 Bangladesh cyclone.

Better weather satellites have been a big help in keeping people safe. Satellites take pictures of storms. They send the pictures to weather forecasters back on Earth. Weather satellites have been spotting hurricanes since the 1960s. But in those days, satellites could spot hurricanes only after they had already formed. In modern times, satellites can alert meteorologists before a hurricane starts. Sensors on the satellites can measure water temperatures, winds, and other weather conditions that often cause hurricanes. With this information, forecasters can keep watch as hurricanes form. They can then send out early alerts if a severe storm develops.

GOOD LINKS

The Emergency Email Network
http://www.emergencyemail.org
Sign up for automatic e-mail alerts about hurricanes and other emergencies. They are free at this neat website.

National Hurricane Center
http://www.nhc.noaa.gov
The National Hurricane Center has the latest lists of new storms. It includes their paths and images taken from satellites and with radar.

In the future, weather satellites may gather more information about the winds that steer hurricanes. These winds often determine whether a hurricane will cause a disaster. A disaster may happen if the winds steer a hurricane toward land. But if the winds carry the hurricane out into the ocean, then the storm will not endanger people.

WATCHING EVERY STEP

Once a storm has formed, meteorologists can watch it every minute. Heat sensors on satellites can spot patches of warm or cold ocean water in a storm's path. Warm water pumps up a storm's energy. It can make the storm grow stronger.

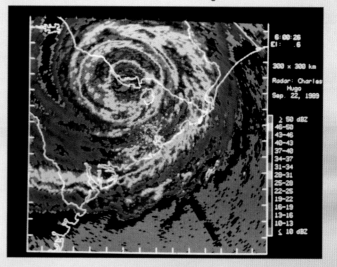

A radar image of Hurricane Hugo (1989) shows the storm was still quite dangerous even after it had traveled far inland.

50

"More than a thousand people lost their lives as a result of these hurricanes, and millions more were left battered, broken, displaced, or homeless."

—An American Red Cross report on the record-breaking 2005 Atlantic hurricane season

Hurricane Katrina evacuees arrive at the New Orleans Superdome after extensive flooding in 2005 forced them from their homes.

Cold water will sap a storm's energy. It will make the storm weaken. Winds at the right height above the ocean can blow a hurricane apart.

Special computer programs, called models, help forecasters guess where the storm will make landfall. They also show how strong a hurricane will be and the amount of damage people can expect. Weather forecasters must use several models to decide whether a hurricane will land and where. That is because none of the models are 100 percent correct.

HURRICANES AND YOUR PETS

When Hurricane Katrina raced toward the Gulf coast in 2005, many people had to evacuate without their pets. Most shelters did not allow animals. Some people refused to leave without their pets. These people faced dangerous situations when the hurricane hit.

In the future, more shelters may allow pets. But in the meantime, pet owners should come up with a plan to protect their animals in an emergency. With just a little planning, you *can* bring your pet with you if you have to evacuate.

Start by making a list of hotels where pets are allowed. That way, you'll have a place to stay even if you can't go to a shelter. You also can talk to friends and family members to see if they would be willing to house your pet in an emergency.

It's also a good idea to prepare a disaster supply kit for your pet. Include enough food and water for three days. If you have a cat, be sure to pack a litter box. The kit should also include your pet's carrier, medicines, a first aid kit, and medical records. Bring a photo in case your pet gets lost, and be sure the animal is wearing a license tag.

A weather forecaster compares weather
patterns and models on several computers.

In the future, meteorologists will have better models. The models will process millions more pieces of information about a hurricane. So forecasters may someday have a model that predicts exactly how a hurricane will act.

BETTER PREDICTIONS

Getting accurate information on storms is important to people living in hurricane country. When people know that a strong hurricane is coming, they can prepare for the storm. They also may have more time to leave the area.

Hurricane predictions are about twice as accurate in modern times as in the past. In the 1970s, meteorologists could predict three days in advance that a hurricane would make landfall somewhere within a 450-mile (724 km) area. By the early 2000s, they could predict landfall to within 200 miles (322 km). Predictions one day ahead of landfall were accurate to within 85 miles (137 km). In the future, these predictions may be accurate to within 10 or 20 miles (16 to 32 km). The more accurate hurricane predictions are, the safer people will be from disasters.

HURRICANE SUPPLY KIT

If you live in hurricane country, help your family prepare a hurricane supply kit. Check the kit before the start of each hurricane season. Replace stale supplies. Be sure to include the following items in your kit:

- Bottled water for each person and pet. Include at least 3 gallons (11 liters) per person per day.

- Canned food (and a can opener) and packaged food that does not need to be refrigerated

- First aid kit and prescription medicines

- Flashlights, a portable radio, and extra batteries

- Raincoats, bedding, or sleeping bags

- A copy of the homeowners or renters insurance policy

- Special items for infants, elderly family members, and pets

Take the kit along if you have to evacuate your home. Try to bring some cash and credit cards that will work for charging gasoline and any motel rooms and meals.

Timeline

1495   Christopher Columbus writes the first known report of a hurricane.

1703   A severe hurricane devastates southern Great Britain.

1715   A fleet of Spanish treasure ships sinks off the coast of Florida.

1780   A giant hurricane kills approximately 22,000 people in the Caribbean.

1881   A typhoon hits Vietnam, killing about 300,000 people.

1882   A cyclone in the Arabian Sea, near Bombay, India, drowns more than 100,000 people.

1900   A hurricane ravages Galveston, Texas. The storm demolishes the city and kills more than 8,000 people.

1928   Around 2,000 people drown when a hurricane strikes Lake Okeechobee, Florida.

1938   A September hurricane strikes New England and causes tremendous damage *(left)*.

1942   A cyclone in the Bay of Bengal causes the deaths of around 40,000 people in Calcutta, India.

1953   A typhoon destroys approximately one-third of Nagoya, Japan.

1955   The damage from Hurricane Diane causes $3.25 billion in damage to the New England area of the United States.

1963   Hurricane Flora hits the Dominican Republic and Haiti. The storm kills 7,190 people.

1969   Herbert Saffir and Robert Simpson develop the Saffir-Simpson Hurricane Scale to measure the strength of hurricanes.

          Hurricane Camille *(right)* hits the United States.

1970   A cyclone hits Bangladesh, killing about 300,000 people.

1988   Hurricane Gilbert *(left)* arrives in Jamaica with 145-mile-per hour (233 km/hr) winds.

1991   Bangladesh loses more than 130,000 people in a violent cyclone.

1992   Hurricane Andrew arrives in Florida and causes billions of dollars in property damage.

1998   Hurricane Mitch brings extensive rainfall, affecting more than 2 million people in Central America.

2004   Charley, Frances *(right)*, Ivan, and Jeanne hit the United States, marking the first time since 1886 that four hurricanes struck in one year.

2005   The Atlantic sees more hurricanes than in any other year since record keeping began.

Hurricane Katrina slams into the Gulf coast, flooding New Orleans and forcing about 1 million people to evacuate.

Hurricane Stan hits the coasts of Mexico and Central America, causing mudslides and large-scale destruction.

Glossary

cyclone: the name for a hurricane that forms near Australia or in the Indian Ocean

dropwindsonde: instruments dropped inside a hurricane to take measurements of the storm. The instruments tell scientists about the wind speed, temperature, and atmospheric pressure inside a hurricane.

evacuate: to leave a dangerous area and go somewhere safe

eye: a hurricane's core. It is very calm in the middle of the eye.

eyewall: a bank of swirling clouds that surrounds the center of a hurricane

global warming: an increase in Earth's temperature due to air pollution

landfall: to come onto shore

meteorologist: a scientist who studies the weather

rainband: bands of clouds that move across an area affected by a hurricane

Saffir-Simpson Hurricane Scale: a scale for measuring hurricanes. The Saffir-Simpson Hurricane Scale assigns a category, or number, to each hurricane. A Category 1 storm is the weakest, while a Category 5 is the strongest.

satellite: a small, unmanned spacecraft that circles high above Earth's surface. Satellites take photographs of storms and send the pictures down to Earth.

storm surge: a dome of water that a hurricane sucks up from the ocean. When a hurricane reaches land, water from the storm surge flows very quickly over everything in its path.

tropical depression: a low-pressure area surrounded by winds that spin in circles. When the wind in a tropical depression goes above 38 miles per hour (61 km/hr), the depression becomes a tropical storm.

typhoon: the name for a hurricane that forms near the Philippines or in the China Sea

water vapor: water in gas form. Water vapor is created when liquid water evaporates.

Places to Visit

The Children's Museum of History, Natural History, Science & Technology—Utica, New York
http://www.museum4kids.net
This museum is home to the Weather Room, where you can explore many interactive exhibits.

The Galveston County Historical Museum—Galveston, Texas
http://www.galveston.com/museums/gchm.shtm
At this museum, you can view original film footage of the 1900 hurricane that devastated the city.

The Imaginarium Hands-On Museum—Fort Myers, Florida
http://www.cityftmyers.com/attractions/imaginarium.aspx
The Imaginarium has a hurricane exhibit where you can feel the effects of hurricane winds on your body. You can also pretend to be a weather newscaster in the museum's weather studio.

Source Notes

4 Debra Englehart, quoted in Jamie Fessler, "OLA Is Temporary School for Hurricane Katrina Victim," *ColumbiaLedger.com*, September 29, 2005, http://www.zwire.com/site/news.cfm?newsid=15302280&BRD=2246&PAG=461&dept_id=452816&rfi=6 (October 17, 2005).

5 Adele Bertucci, "New Orleans: Survivor Stories," *CityPages.com*, September 20, 2005, http://www.citypages.com/databank/26/1294/article13694.asp?page=2 (October 28, 2005).

7 Robert Moss, quoted in Chris Wadsworth, "Andrew Left Scars, Lessons," *news-press.com*, January 2, 2003, http://www.news-press.com/news/weather/hurricane/stories/040822andrew.html (January 18, 2006).

8 Helen McCormick, quoted in Liz Doup, "1928—Okeechobee: The Night 2,000 Died," *SunSentinal.com*, September 11, 1988, http://www.sun-sentinel.com/news/weather/hurricane/sfl-1928-hurricane,0,2734526.story (October 28, 2005).

12 NEMO Secretariat, "Saint Lucia: NEMO Remembers the Great Hurricane of 1780," *CDERA*, October 7, 2005, http://www.cdera.org/cunews/news/saint_lucia/printer_1314.php (November 14, 2005).

12 Ibid.

13 Ibid.

21 Mike Spencer, quoted in Mike Brunker, "Survivors Tell of Desperate Struggles to Survive," *MSNBC*, August 30, 2005, http://www.msnbc.msn.com/id/9129659/ (January 18, 2006).

23 Ida Smith Austin, quoted in Galveston Newspapers, Inc., "Through a Night of Horrors," *The 1900 Storm*, 2005, http://www.1900storm.com/nightofhorrors/index.lasso (October 7, 2005).

23 Isaac M. Cline, "Special Report on the Galveston Hurricane of September 8, 1900," *NOAA History*, February 4, 2004, http://www.history.noaa.gov/stories_tales/cline2.html (October 7, 2005).

23 Casey Edward Greene and Shelly Henley Kelly, eds., *Through a Night of Horrors: Voices from the 1900 Galveston Storm*. (College Station: Texas A&M University Press, 2003), 16.

23 Ibid.

24 Bill Wotkutch, quoted in Traci Watson, "Ivan Drenching Dooms Pa. Towns," *USA Today*, September 20, 2004, http://www.usatoday.com/weather/hurricane/2004-09-20-hurricane-inside_x.htm (October 7, 2005).

28 Arthur Raynor, quoted in *The 1938 Hurricane As We Remember It: Volume II* (East Patchogue, NY: Searles Graphics, Inc., 1998). Also available online at "The Long Island Express," http://www2.sunysuffolk.edu/mandias/38hurricane/human_interest.html (October 7, 2005).

28 Ibid.

29 Richard K. Hawes, *The Hurricane at Westport Harbor* (Fall River, MA: The Dover Press, 1938), quoted in "Westport (MA) History," *The Westport Historical Society*, September 19, 2003, http://www.westporthistory.com/news/archives/000125.html (October 31, 2005).

29 Ibid.

31 Marian Acuna Cruz, quoted in *Reuters Foundation AlertNet*, "Eyewitness: Hurricane Mitch—Five Years On," October 31, 2003, http://www.alertnet.org/thefacts/reliefresources/106759809664.htm (January 19, 2006).

37 Asel Haider, quoted in Mark Levine, "A Storm at the Bone: A Personal Exploration into Deep Weather," *Outside*, November 1998, http://outside.away.com/outside/magazine/1198/9811storm.html (October 31, 2005).

37 Jotish Chandra Koibarta, quoted in Gilles Saussier, "Dancing with the Rivers—Bangladeshi Settlements Built on Chars," *UNESCO Courier*, July–August 1999, http://www.findarticles.com/p/articles/mi_m1310/is_1999_July-August/ai_55413352/print (October 31, 2005).

40 Michael Benitez, quoted in "Hurricane: Storm Science," *Miami Museum of Science*, 2000, http://www.miamisci.org/hurricane/meetmichael.html (October 7, 2005).

40 Marilyn Wallace, quoted in "CJ Experience: Hurricane Katrina," *MSNBC.com*, September 28, 2005, http://www.msnbc.msn.com/id/9076525/print/1/displaymode/1098 (October 31, 2005).

40 Philip D. Hearn, *Hurricane Camille: Monster Storm of the Gulf Coast* (Jackson: University Press of Mississippi, 2004), 160.

44 Abby Maxman, quoted in "Overseas Work: Three Quarters of Flood-Affected Haitians Still Waiting for Food and Water," *Care International*, n.d., http://www.careinternational.org.uk/cares_work/where/haiti/media_releases/media_release.php?id=333 (October 31, 2005).

45 Louna Registe, quoted in Maite Alvarez, "Eyewitness: Amid Haiti's Filth and Grief," *BBC News*, September 24, 2004, http://news.bbc.co.uk/1/hi/world/americas/3687226.stm (January 19, 2006).

47 Raul Murillo, quoted in Edgar Calderon, "Tropical Storm Stan Kills at Least 225 in Central America, Mexico," *Agence France-Presse*, October 7, 2005, http://www.reliefweb.int/rw/RWB.NSF/db900SID/VBOL6GXCWC?OpenDocument (October 31, 2005).

47 Carlos Rosales, quoted in "'In Some Cases Entire Communities Have Been Destroyed . . .'—an Eyewitness Account from Guatemala," *Christian Aid*, October 2005, http://www.christian-aid.org.uk/crisis/central%20america/interview2.htm (October 31, 2005).

47 Beatriz Aguilar, quoted in "'It Rained Entire Rivers'—an Eyewitness Account from El Salvador," *Christian Aid*, October 2005, http://www.christian-aid.org.uk/crisis/central%20america/interview1.htm (October 31, 2005).

48 Monowar Hossain Akhand, "Disaster Management and Cyclone Warning System in Bangladesh," *GFZ Potsdam*, n.d., http://www.gfz-potsdam.de/ewc98/abstract/akhand.html (October 31, 2005).

51 *American Red Cross*, "Hurricane Season 2005: A Season in Review," n.d., http://www.redcross.org/news/ds/hurricanes/2005 (January 19, 2005).

Selected Bibliography

Allaby, Michael. *A Chronology of Weather: Dangerous Weather*. New York: Facts on File, Inc., 1998.

Cattermole, Peter, and Stuart Clark. "Hurricanes and Tornadoes." *New Encyclopedia of Science. Earth and Other Planets: Geology and Space Research*. New York: Oxford University Press, 2003.

Davies, Peter. *Inside the Hurricane: Face to Face with Nature's Deadliest Storms*. New York: Henry Holt and Company, 2000.

Gorman, Jeff. *Atlas of Natural Disasters*. New York: Michael Friedman Publishing Group, 2002.

Larson, Erik. *Isaac's Storm: A Man, a Time, and the Deadliest Hurricane in History*. New York: Crown Publishing, 1999.

Longshore, David. *Encyclopedia of Hurricanes, Typhoons and Cyclones*. New York: Facts on File, Inc., 1998.

Sheets, Bob. *Hurricane Watch: Forecasting the Deadliest Storms on Earth*. New York: Random House, 2001.

Williams, John M., and Iver W. Duedall. *Florida Hurricanes and Tropical Storms, 1871–2001*. Gainesville: University Press of Florida, 2002.

Further Resources

BOOKS

Anderson, Laurie Halse. *Storm Rescue*. Milwaukee: Gareth Stevens Publishing, 2003. This novel tells the story of Sunita, a girl who must overcome her fear of storms in order to rescue a stranded cat.

Brennan, Kristine. *The Galveston Hurricane*. Philadelphia: Chelsea House Publishers, 2002. When the hurricane of 1900 descends on Galveston, Texas, it destroys the city and takes many lives.

Challen, Paul. *Hurricane and Typhoon Alert!* New York: Crabtree Publishing Company, 2004. This title explores the science behind hurricanes and includes an experiment you can try.

Cole, Joanna. *The Magic School Bus: Inside a Hurricane*. New York: Scholastic, 1995. Follow Ms. Frizzle as she takes her busload of students into the eye of a hurricane.

Demarest, Chris L.. *Hurricane Hunters!: Riders on the Storm*. New York: Margaret McElderry Books, 2006. Learn how hurricane hunters study hurricanes by flying into the storms.

Sherrow, Victoria. *Hurricane Andrew: Nature's Rage*. Springfield, NJ: Enslow, 1998. This title discusses the effects of Hurricane Andrew and the recovery effort that followed the storm.

Simon, Seymour. *Hurricanes*. New York: HarperCollins, 2003. Simon presents an explanation of hurricanes and why they develop as well as advice on remaining safe during a hurricane.

Trueit, Trudi Strain. *Storm Chasers*. New York: Franklin Watts, 2002. Read all about the exciting work of meteorologists and others who study storms.

Warner, Gertrude Chandler. *The Hurricane Mystery*. Morton Grove, IL.: Albert Whitman & Co., 1996. The Boxcar children are in South Carolina after a hurricane, helping their neighbor with repairs, when they come upon a mystery.

Woods, Michael, and Mary B. Woods. *Tornadoes*. Minneapolis: Lerner Publications Company, 2007. Find out about some of the world's most destructive tornadoes.

WEBSITES AND FILMS

AccuSchool: Hurricane Center

http://www.accuweather.com/wx/school/hurricane.htm

This site includes hurricane facts, a description of the components that make up hurricanes, an explanation of how hurricanes form, and a list of Atlantic storm names.

A Fierce Force of Nature: Hurricanes

http://observe.arc.nasa.gov/nasa/earth/hurricane/intro.html

This site explains how hurricanes begin, when and where hurricanes hit, how scientists track hurricanes, and what to do if a hurricane is heading toward you.

Flying Into the Eye of a . . . Hurricane!

http://www.nationalgeographic.com/ngkids/0308/hurricane

Visit this site to learn more about hurricane hunters, read fascinating facts about hurricanes, and find useful hurricane safety tips.

Frequently Asked Questions: Hurricanes

http://www.aoml.noaa.gov/hrd/tcfaq/tcfaqHED.html

This page from the National Oceanic and Atmospheric Administration answers all your questions about hurricanes.

Hurricane: Storm Science

http://www.miamisci.org/hurricane/index.html

This page from the Miami Museum of Science includes information on weather instruments, hurricane tracking, storm survivors, and more.

The Hurricane Hunters

http://www.hurricanehunters.com

The 53rd Weather Reconnaissance Squadron maintains this site with pictures and information about recent hurricanes.

Hurricanes

http://www.fema.gov/kids/hurr.htm

This site provides extensive information on hurricanes and includes interactive games.

Hurricanes: The Greatest Storms on Earth

http://earthobservatory.nasa.gov/Library/Hurricanes

This detailed site explains storm surge, the Saffir-Simpson Hurricane Scale, the anatomy of a hurricane, and more.

The 1900 Storm

http://www.1900storm.com

Find out about this storm that swept through Galveston, Texas.

University of Illinois: Hurricanes Online Meteorology Guide

http://ww2010.atmos.uiuc.edu/(Gh)/guides/mtr/hurr/home.rxml

Fly through a hurricane with 3-D video.

Hurricane! Boston: NOVA, 2004.

In this DVD, you can learn about hurricanes Gilbert and Camille and follow scientists as they fly into hurricanes.

Nature's Fury. United States: National Geographic, 2000.

This DVD explores many types of extreme weather, including hurricanes, floods, and tornadoes.

Index

Photo Acknowledgments

The photos in this book are used with the permission of: Jocelyn Augustino/FEMA, pp. 1, 51; Courtesy of the National Oceanic and Atmospheric Administration Central Library Photo Collection, pp. 3, 14, 15, 28, 29, 31, 33, 34, 50, 55; © HENRY ROMERO/Reuters/CORBIS, p. 4; © Louis DeLuca/Dallas Morning News/CORBIS, p. 5; © The Mariners' Museum/CORBIS, p. 6; © Najlah Feanny/CORBIS SABA, p. 7; © Lannis Waters/Palm Beach Post/ZUMA Press, p. 8; © DANIEL LECLAIR/Reuters/CORBIS, p. 9; © Charles W. Luzier/Reuters/CORBIS, pp. 10, 30; © Smiley N. Pool/Dallas Morning News/CORBIS, p. 11; © age footstock/SuperStock, pp. 12, 39, 53; © Hulton Archive/Getty Images, p. 13; © Reuters/CORBIS, p. 16; © Bettmann/CORBIS, pp. 17, 40, 56 (bottom); NASA, p. 18 (both); Library of Congress, pp. 19, 22 (LC-USZ62-123886), 23 (LC-USZ62-56437), p. 42 (LC-USZ62-108564); Bob Epstein/FEMA, p. 20; Michael Rieger/FEMA, p. 21; Mark Wolfe/FEMA, p. 24; © Mike Theiss/Jim Reed Photography/CORBIS, p. 32; © Jim Edds/Jim Reed Photography/CORBIS, p. 35; © Pablo Bartholomew/Liaison Agency/Getty Images, p.p 36, 37, 49; © Stan Honda/AFP/Getty Images, p. 38; © Jose Azel/Aurora/Getty Images, p. 41; © CARLOS BARRIA/Reuters/CORBIS, p. 43; © RICK WILKING/ Reuters/CORBIS, p. 44 (left); © Michael Macor/San Francisco Chronicle/CORBIS, p. 44 (right); AP/Wide World Photos, p. 45; © STR/AFT/Getty Images, p. 46; © ORLANDO SIERRA/AFP/Getty Images, p. 47 (left); © YURI CORTEZ/AFP/Getty Images, p. 47 (right); Sally McGraw, 2003, p. 52 (top); Courtesy of Jessica Puckett, p. 52 (bottom); © Keystone/Hulton Archive/Getty Images, p. 56 (top); © Sergio Donantes/CORBIS, p. 57 (top); © Jon Davies/Jim Reed Photography/CORBIS, p. 57 (bottom). Diagram by Bill Hauser, p. 19.

Front Cover: AP/Wide World Photos, Back Cover: Liz Roll/FEMA.

About the Authors

Michael Woods is a science and medical journalist in Washington, D.C., who has won many national writing awards. He works in the National Bureau of the *Pittsburgh Post-Gazette* and the *Toledo Blade*. Mary B. Woods has been a librarian in the Fairfax County Public School System in Virginia and the Benjamin Franklin International School in Barcelona, Spain. Their previous books include the eight-volume Ancient Technology series. The Woodses have four children. When not writing, reading, or enjoying their two grand-children, the Woodses travel to gather material for future books.